Desert

Ellen Labrecque

raintree

Raintree is an imprint of Capstone Global Library Limited, a company incorporated in England and Wales having its registered office at 7 Pilgrim Street, London, EC4V 6LB – Registered company number: 6695582

www.raintree.co.uk
myorders@raintree.co.uk

Edited by James Benefield and Brenda Haugen
Designed by Richard Parker
Original illustrations © Capstone Global Library Ltd 2015
Picture research by Jo Miller
Production by Helen McCreath
Originated by Capstone Global Library Ltd
Printed and bound in China

ISBN 978 1 406 28775 2 (hardback)
18 17 16 15 14
10 9 8 7 6 5 4 3 2 1

ISBN 978 1 406 28782 0 (paperback)
19 18 17 16 15
10 9 8 7 6 5 4 3 2 1

British Library Cataloguing in Publication Data
A full catalogue record for this book is available from the British Library.

Acknowledgments
We would like to thank the following for permission to reproduce photographs: Alamy: Barry Iverson, 21, Johner Images, 23, Robert Estall photo agency, 13; Corbis: Bob Krist, 18; Newscom: Arco Images/picture alliance/K.Kreder, 17, Danita Delimont Photography/Alison Wright, 12, Getty Images/AFP/Greg Wood, 19, Getty Images/AFP/Jamal Nasrallah, 22, Oliver Gerhard Image Broker, 11, Robert Harding/Tuul, 15, ZUMA Press/Du Boisberranger, 14; Pascal Maitre, 27; Shutterstock: apinunrin, 24, ChameleonsEye, 25, devy, cover, grebcha, 5, JuRitt, 4, Nataliya Hora, 26, Nicram Sabod, 9, p.studio66, 20, Patrick Poendl, 16, Pi-Lens, 6, prochasson frederic, 8, Xavier MARCHANT, 10.

Design Elements: Shutterstock: donatas1205, Olympus.

We would like to thank Rachel Bowles for her invaluable help in the preparation of this book.

Every effort has been made to contact copyright holders of material reproduced in this book. Any omissions will be rectified in subsequent printings if notice is given to the publisher.

All the internet addresses (URLs) given in this book were valid at the time of going to press. However, due to the dynamic nature of the internet, some addresses may have changed, or sites may have changed or ceased to exist since publication. While the author and publisher regret any inconvenience this may cause readers, no responsibility for any such changes can be accepted by either the author or the publisher.

Contents

Some words are shown in bold, **like this**. You can find out what they mean by looking in the glossary.

What is a desert?

Deserts are places on Earth that get little rainfall. Deserts get less than 25 centimetres (around 10 inches) of **precipitation** a year. Deserts can be hot or cold, but many are hot during the day and cooler at night.

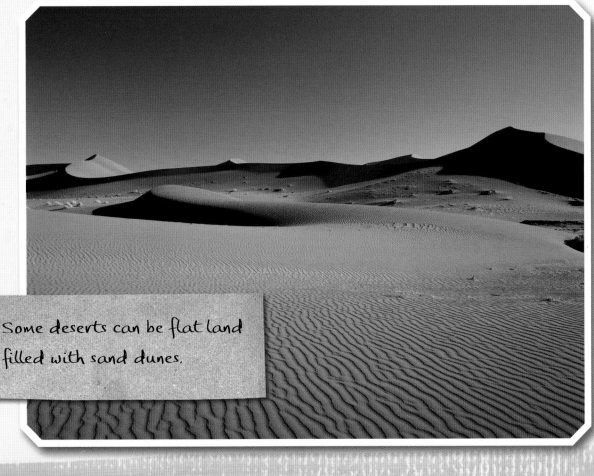

Some deserts can be flat land filled with sand dunes.

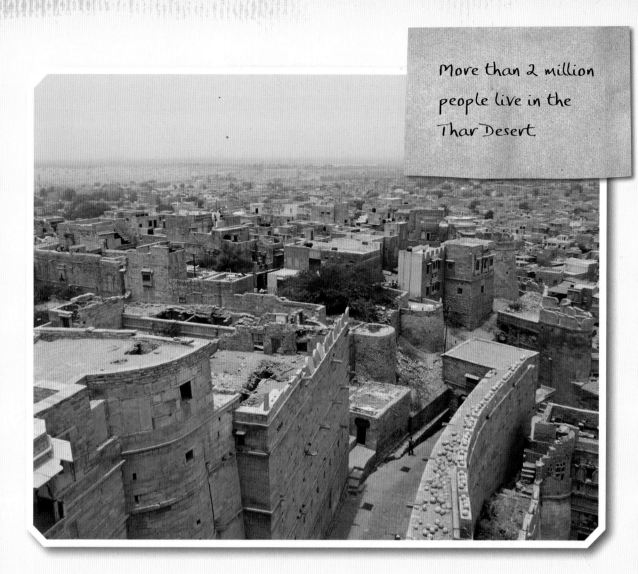

Some deserts have few people living in them. Other deserts have lots of people living in **settlements**. More people live in the Thar Desert in India and Pakistan than live in any other hot desert in the world.

Where are deserts?

Deserts are found on every **continent**, and where there is little rain. The world's largest desert is the Antarctic Desert. It is made entirely of ice and almost nobody lives there.

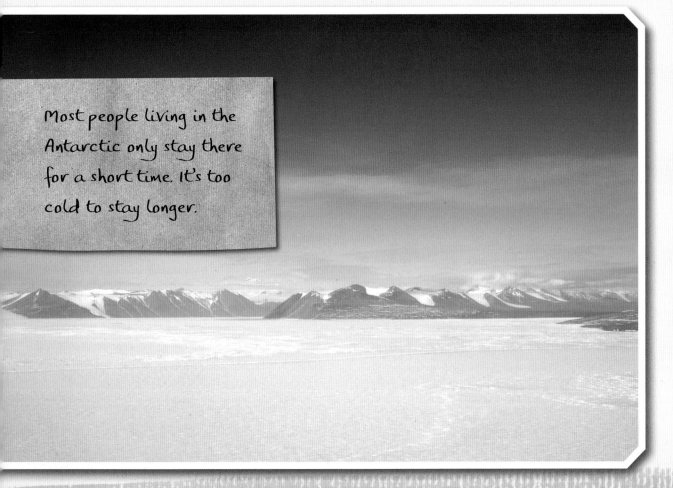

Most people living in the Antarctic only stay there for a short time. It's too cold to stay longer.

The world's largest hot desert is the Sahara Desert.

Arctic Desert

Gobi Desert

Sahara Desert

Arabian Desert

Deserts start near mountains, where clouds from the sea are stopped from moving inland by these mountains. Or, deserts start where there is high **air pressure**, which stops the rain. They can also form along the coast. When warm air meets cold seas, it stops rain from coming inland.

Earth's largest deserts

1. Antarctic Desert
2. Arctic Desert
3. Sahara Desert, Northern Africa
4. Arabian Desert, Southwest Asia
5. Gobi Desert, Central Asia

All kinds of people

Over 1 billion people live in deserts. Most of them live in cities. Cities have lots of places to work, from shops to offices. People avoid the sun and sandstorms by staying inside.

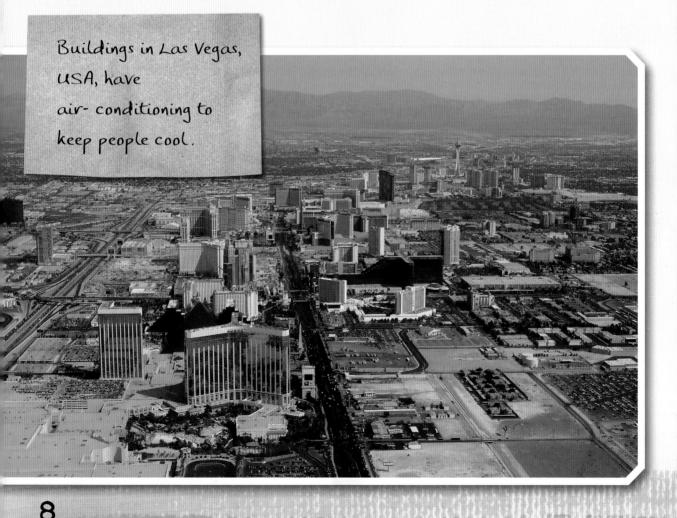

Buildings in Las Vegas, USA, have air-conditioning to keep people cool.

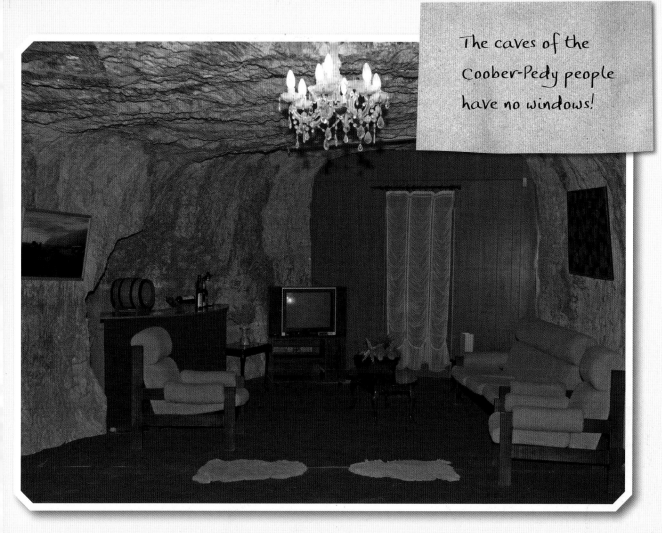

The caves of the Coober-Pedy people have no windows!

Other people live in different ways. In Africa, some people live in mud huts in the desert. In the desert in Coober-Pedy, Australia, some people live in caves. The caves help them stay cool inside when it is hot outside.

Living in the desert

Living in the desert is tough. There is not enough rain to grow **crops**. Food and water are brought to desert cities from far away. Many desert people live near an **oasis**, where they get their water from wells.

Two-thirds of the people in the Sahara Desert get their water from wells in an oasis.

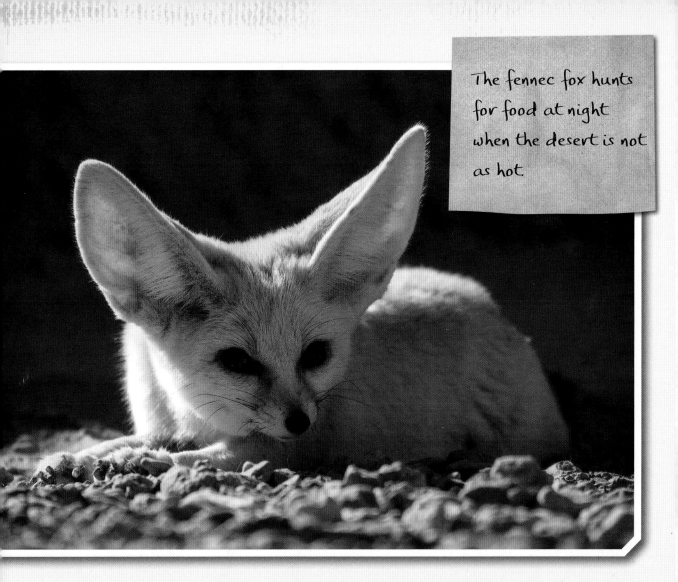

The fennec fox hunts for food at night when the desert is not as hot

Bad weather also makes desert living hard. High winds whip up sandstorms. Dust fills the air and makes it hard to see or breathe. The animals that live there sleep during the day and roam at night.

Who are nomads?

Nomads move their homes from place to place. This is because they move around looking for food and water. Nomads can also travel with their own animals, such as goats and sheep.

Nomads in the Gobi Desert sleep in tents called yurts. Yurts are light to carry and easy to set up.

The Sans people suck up water through a straw.

Some nomads have unusual ways to find water. In the Kalahari Desert, Sans nomads find water under the sand. They store it in ostrich egg shells!

Weather and clothes

In hot deserts, people wear light, loose clothes. This helps them to stay cool. People wear clothes to protect themselves too. The Tuareg people in Africa cover their whole head with a piece of material called a **veil**.

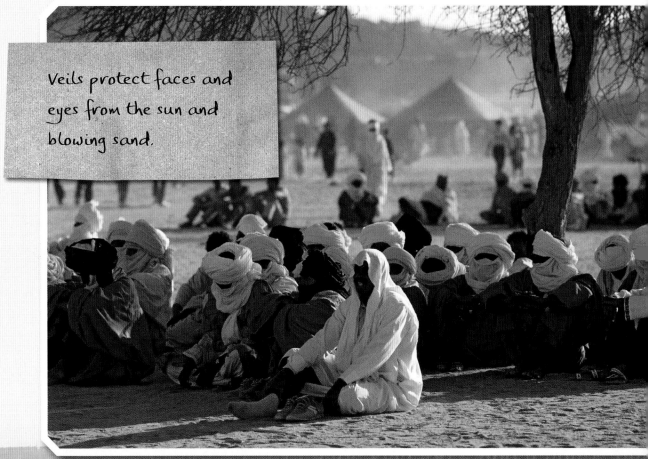

Veils protect faces and eyes from the sun and blowing sand.

A deel can be used as a blanket. This way, nomads don't have to carry a separate blanket.

In cold deserts, people wear many layers. **Nomads** in the Gobi Desert wear long robes called deels over other warm clothes. Deels are warm as they are made from sheepskin.

Getting around

Today, you can travel around most deserts in cars and trucks. Some people drive their cars off the roads. They need to be careful they don't get stuck in the sand or lost.

People should bring their own supply of food, water and petrol when they travel across deserts.

A camel's feet are flat and wide. This means it doesn't sink into the sand when it walks.

Many **nomads** still travel on camels in hot deserts. Camels are the perfect animal for desert travel. They have long eyelashes that help to keep sand out of their eyes. They can also go for days without food or water.

What is school like?

Some children in the desert go to schools like yours. Others stay at home and their mum or dad teaches them. Some children in the desert have to walk many miles to get to school.

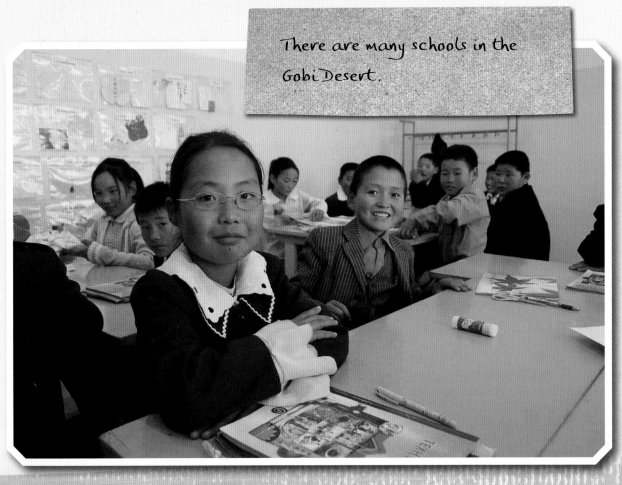

There are many schools in the Gobi Desert.

Children who live in the Outback of Australia use School of the Air. At a School of the Air, children learn at home. They listen to a teacher on a radio or watch them on a video link, using the internet.

What is work like?

Some jobs in deserts are just like jobs anywhere else. Grown-ups can be doctors or teachers and live in a desert. Sometimes, just looking for food and water in the desert is a big job! But some desert jobs are special.

Some people in deserts have jobs just like the grown-ups you know.

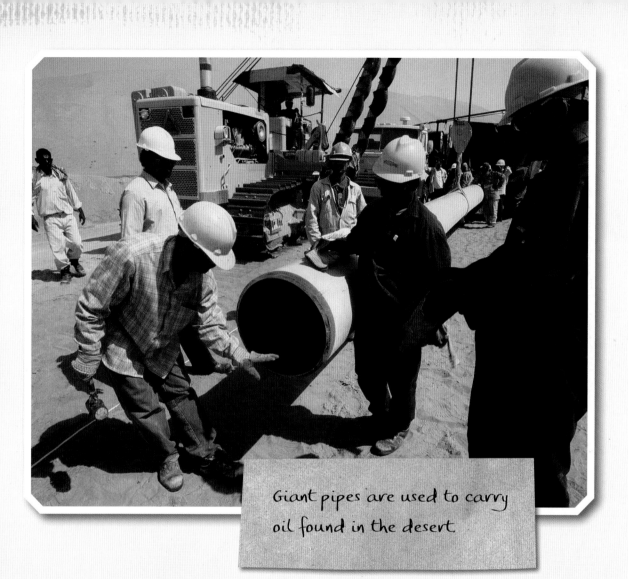

Giant pipes are used to carry oil found in the desert.

Much of the world's oil is found underneath the Arabian deserts. Workers pump the oil from the ground using special machines. Oil has many uses. For example, it can be turned into petrol for vehicles.

Fun things to do

There are amazing events in deserts. Some flat deserts are perfect for speed events. The land speed record is the highest speed reached by a car. It was set in 1997 at the Black Rock Desert in the USA at 1,227 kilometres (763 miles) per hour!

The ThrustSSC set the land speed record.

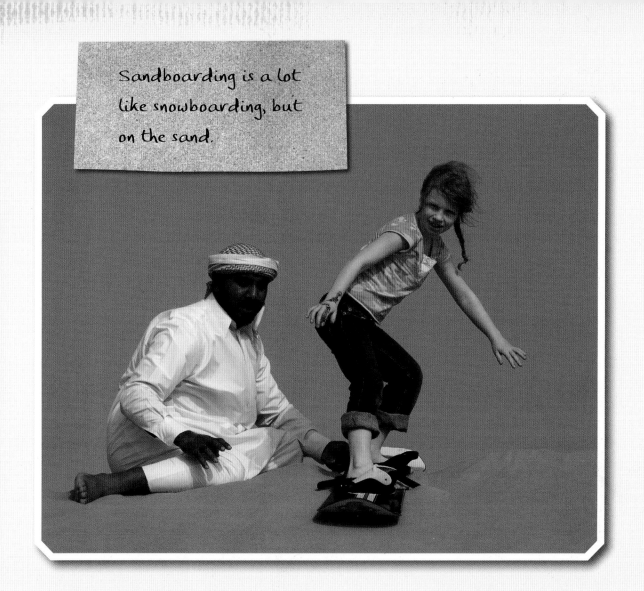

Sandboarding is a lot like snowboarding, but on the sand.

Many people take holidays in the desert. They enjoy the hot weather and the sights. You can stay in fancy hotels with swimming pools in the Arabian Desert in Western Asia. You can try sports, such as sandboarding, in the desert.

Deserts of the past

People have lived in deserts for thousands of years. But desert living has changed a lot. Thousands of years ago, the dry land that is now the Sahara Desert used to have lakes!

Some scientists think **climate change** has made grass, rivers and lakes disappear.

People have also found dinosaur bones, fossilized eggs and other fossils in the desert.

Archaeologists work in deserts to find out things about the past. They have found buildings, ancient drawings and **artefacts**, such as pottery, beneath the sand.

Deserts of the future

Some scientists say **climate change** is changing deserts. Some deserts grow bigger as land gets less rain. Other deserts grow because of **deforestation**. Without trees, land and soil dries out and blows away.

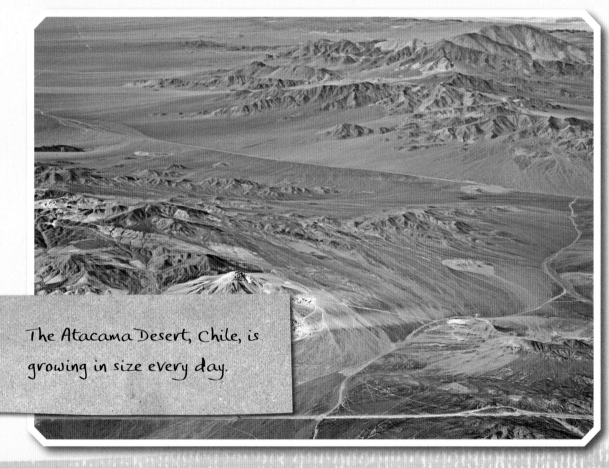

The Atacama Desert, Chile, is growing in size every day.

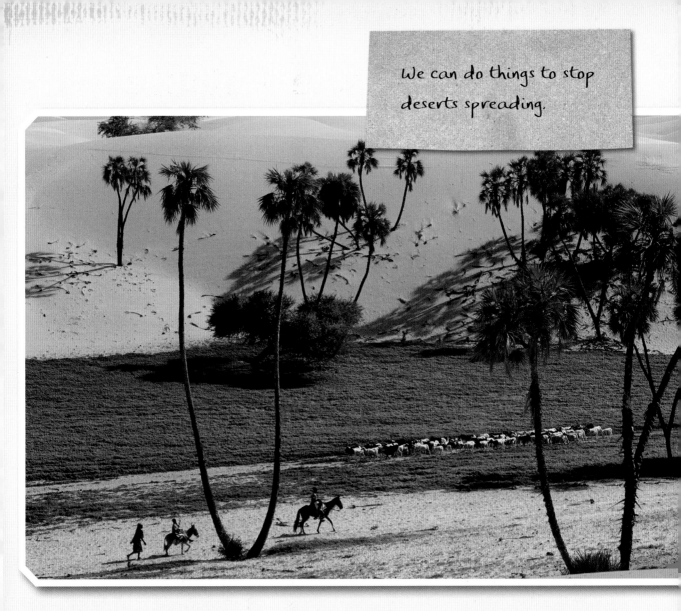

We can do things to stop deserts spreading.

People are learning to cut back on air pollution from factories and vehicles that some scientists think could cause climate change. People are also trying to **conserve** water.

Fun facts

- Deserts have been around for millions of years.

- The most common plants in US deserts are cacti. They are tough plants that have a waxy stem that holds water.

- Many reptiles live in the desert. Their scaly skin stops them from drying out in the heat.

- Most of the animals that live in hot deserts live underground!

- Sometimes, tired and thirsty desert travellers see mirages of water. A mirage looks like shimmering water up ahead, but it is really just a trick (or illusion) caused by light from the Sun. An illusion is something we think is real, but is not actually there.

Quiz

Are each of these sentences true or false?

1. All deserts are hot and sandy.
2. There are no cities in the desert.
3. More land is turning into desert all the time.
4. A horse is the perfect animal to ride on in the desert.
5. It is best to wear tight-fitting clothes in the desert.

5. False. Loose-fitting clothes keep you cool and protect you from the Sun.

4. False. A camel is one of the best animals to travel through the desert on.

3. True. Deserts are growing every day. Some think this is because the world grows hotter and hotter.

2. False. There are many cities in the desert. Supplies are brought in from other places.

1. False. Deserts can be cold and icy. They can be rocky and full of mountains, too.

Glossary

air pressure forces that push and pull, which happen all around us, in the air we breathe. Different forces cause different weather!

archaeologist person who studies ancient people by digging up buildings and things from long ago

artefacts old object made by a person. They tell us about life in a particular time.

climate change long lasting change in the weather. Some scientists think it happens because of people causing pollution.

conserve slow down or stop something from disappearing

continent any of the world's big land areas: Africa, Antarctica, Asia, Australia, Europe, North America and South America

crops plants grown for food

deforestation cutting down of trees and big plants. Sometimes caused by having too many farm animals eating grass and plants.

nomad person who has no long lasting home. They travel from place to place to find food, water and places to graze animals.

oasis spot in a desert where water and plants are found

precipitation mist, rain, snow, hail or sleet that falls to the ground

settlement place where people's homes are, such as a village, town or city

veil material that covers a face. In deserts, it protects a person from sandstorms and from the Sun.

Find out more

Books

Deserts Around the World, Jen Green (Wayland, 2013)

I Wonder Why The Sahara is Cold at Night and other Questions about Deserts, Jackie Gaff (Kingfisher, 2012)

The Atacama Desert (Deserts Around the World), Lynn Peppas (Crabtree Publishing, 2012)

Websites

www.bbc.co.uk/schools/whatisweather
Check out this site to see how people adapt to living with different weather around the world.

http://kids.nationalgeographic.com/explore/countries/ egypt.html
This National Geographic website looks at the country of Egypt, which is mostly desert.

http://pubs.usgs.gov/gip/deserts
You can find great photos of deserts at this US Geological Survey website.

Index